The Heart of a Rose

www.TeresaJamesPoetry.com

The Heart of a Rose

Teresa James

The Heart of a Rose

Copyright © 2021 by Teresa James

The Heart of a Rose

All rights reserved.
No part of this publication may be reproduced or transmitted in any form or by any means electronic or mechanical, including photocopy, recording, or any information storage and retrieval system now known or invented, without permission in writing from the publisher, except by a reviewer who wishes to quote brief passages in connection with a review written for inclusion in a magazine, newspaper, or broadcast.

Paperback ISBN: 978-0-578-94251-3

About Author

Teresa James is known for her poetry and art shared throughout social media as Love of a Poet.
Where you can actually interact with her. She is passionate about the creativity and beauty of poetry. She mostly writes short poems about love and relationships. She is a mother of seven children, a horticulturist, and philanthropist. While going through heartbreaks, struggles, and grief throughout life. She learned to write her emotions down on paper to vent and release pain. She now bleeds ink by writing and sharing through her poetry.

The Heart of a Rose

The Heart of a Rose

I am a Rose of Sharon, a lily of the valleys.
Like a lily among thorns is my darling among the young women.

Song of Songs 2:1-2

The Heart of a Rose

The Heart of a Rose

Prelude

A poem written to me by my dearest friend.

You may see a million other Roses, none really spring to mind. Until you glance upon that Rose who is of the wondrous kind, standing out amongst the crowd. She's the most perfect Rose you've seen.

Her petals lay so perfectly. She surely is a dream elegant and graceful. She holds herself with style, though she knows she's beautiful. She's humble all the while; never trying to out shine those around.

She encourages them to grow, making sure they find their sun. To help their beauty show her tenderness makes her so beguiling, it makes you want her more. If those around her stumble she'll help them up.

She shows all her loving kindness and beauty hiding inside a single Rose. I watch you encourage others and my admiration grows even though you're a stem and half above them. So much prettier than the rest.

I see you guide them to the light to help them be their best. So even though there may be a million Roses so pretty and divine. I was a lucky poet. I found the muse that's mine, so I check on her everyday.

Thinking of her beauty, I try to write in rhyme telling her she's truly amazing. So pretty and so fine. All the other poets you may look upon my special Rose; but there's only one who loves her, I can only hope it shows.

The Heart of a Rose

The Heart of a Rose

CONTENTS

1. Precious Petals………………………………….....…13

2. Piercing the Heart……………………………..……....24

3. Winds of Change……………………………………..36

4. Sounds of Poetry……………………………….....…48

5. A Rose Scorned……………………………….....…..63

6. Moments in Love……………………………………..74

7. Symphony of a Rose……………………………….....86

The Heart of a Rose

Precious Petals

The Heart of a Rose

A rose is the queen of all flowers,
yet guarded by her thorns.

He who desires the benefits of the rose,
must be able to cultivate.

Therefore using skill and wisdom to hold the rose;
without being afraid or harmed by her thorns.

Noble is he who accomplishes,
gathering a rose with charisma.

The Heart of a Rose

I have you—
because I want you,
not because I need you.
I need air to breathe.

Wanting you my love,
is an honor to you.
I have you—
because I want to
keep you near.

The Heart of a Rose

He seeked my attention for some time
I was intrigued although I stayed calm
When I first saw him I knew he was the one
And in my mind is where the romance begun

He took his time to court me well
Even brought me carnations to smell
I learned that chivalry is not dead
A gentleman wears honor upon his head

I remember the first kiss
In our secret place by the lake
Every moment with him is enjoyable
And the walks in the park we partake

Most of all I cherish a special day
When we laid beneath the oak tree
And he kissed me very passionately
Then he reached in his pocket
And gave me a little rose locket

The Heart of a Rose

My soul kisses the
essence of your being.
Your gentleness embraces
me with your soft charm.
Endearing are your ways—
I will remain faithful in love.
As the lily grows in the valley
& the fields dance with the wind.
My love for you will never end.

The Heart of a Rose

If you let me love you
I will show you how it's
truly supposed to be.
I'm sorry your heart is
afraid and trust is far away.

Let me love you and show
you there's a better way.
I will give you the attention
and comfort you need.

I will caress the beauty
you hold within your skin.
Together we will soar high
as our journey begins.
Only if you will let me in.

The Heart of a Rose

Why a Rose?

A rose can say what words may not be able to say.
A rose could simply mean have a nice day.
A rose could say please forgive me in every way.
A rose could comfort feelings and ease dismay.
A rose can say I'm thinking of you today.
A rose can brighten someone who's down.
A rose can make her smile from a sad frown.
A rose can turn someone's grey skies blue.
A rose can say congratulations to you.
A rose can lay your loved one down to rest.
A rose could say I'm sorry for your loss.
A rose could say sorry oops I forgot.
A rose is the queen of all flowers.
A rose will even bloom in the winter.
As the seasons change it seldom withers.

The Heart of a Rose

I've been searching for the words
to tell you how much I miss you.
The way I feel since we parted ways.
And I couldn't quite find them, so…

I went by the little coffee shop we frequented.
Thought about how you used to look my way.
I wanted to approach you and just didn't
know what to say.

Now I can't get you out of my mind
and think about you every day.
A letter seemed too forward and maybe
like I am being eager to please.

So I stopped by the candy shop
to find something sweet.
I saw a sign which displayed "Kind Regards"
so I decided to send you a Postcard.

The Heart of a Rose

The Heart of a Rose

I'm not a one night stand

I will take your hand and
walk you into the depths
of my heart to explore
the valleys of my mind.

I will build you a home in
the shelter of my emotions
while caressing you inside
my sweetness, full of love.

My kiss will take you to
an unfamiliar place and
my touch will show you
the way—come closer.

One night will be forever

Honesty

Trust a pure white rose
As a true symbol of love
A gift of life from above
Never forget to listen to
The sounds of the earth

Time keeps the answers
As the roses scent the air
With sweet love to share
Calming the atmosphere
In the silence we will hear

Truth holds me and you
Embrace the morning dew
Softly enchanting and true
And sadness is never blue
Pure white rose, I adore you

Piercing the Heart

Emotional Abuse

A thief came in the night with
a knife and stabbed me twice.
With words of scrutiny
and emotional blasphemy.
He stole my peace
and even my sense of dignity.
Broke me with the pain of his words.
He stripped me naked and left me
in fear of being exposed.
Gave me roses as a token
but yet once again I'm broken.
Pleasant words can heal
and lethal ones will kill.
How could
    he come into
        my life and
            steal?

The Heart of a Rose

Don't tell me you Love me
Show me what your love can do
Can your love be proven true?
Hold me with integrity
Love me with honesty
Touch me with decency
Caress me with loyalty
Move me with sweet sensitivity
Give me what I desire and need
What exactly are your qualities?
Sway me with accountability
Impress me with your stability
Kiss me with the taste of meekness
Maybe integrity is your weakness?
Don't tell me you Love me
Show me what your love can do

The Heart of a Rose

Cries of a dying rose
Is to weep unseemly
No one sees the tears
Yet she withers away
Holding on to yesterday
When her heart was ok
He who forsakes a rose
A sad lonely price to pay
Love her more everyday

The Heart of a Rose

If words could paint a picture
would you hang mine on your
bedroom wall to be seen?

Would you capture the
abandonment and grief
you bestowed upon me?

Could you center me where
I can receive your attention?
Maybe the emotional
abuse I won't ever mention.

Is there a missing canvas
or just the way you display?
All the missing colors of
my heart that you took away.

The Heart of a Rose

Many sleepless nights have
become a normal part of my life.

As I lay my head on the pillow
with two eyes full of tears.
The love we shared
are now wasted years.

My heart bleeds with
fury as I tell my story.

Why...Oh why,
did this love have to end?
I never thought you'd be the reason
my heart is yearning to mend.

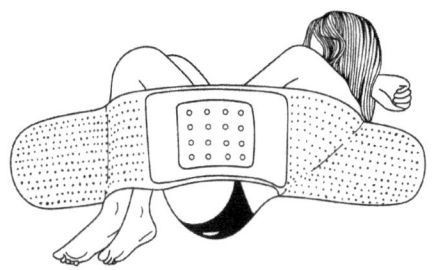

The Heart of a Rose

I was your sun,
moon and the stars.

You were fire,
brimstone and scars.

I was your milky way,
jupiter and mars.

You were the asteroids
blazing very far.

I was your light...
You were my dark.

This galaxy will
keep us apart.

I was never meant
to be your girl.

We are from two
different worlds.

The Heart of a Rose

The Heart of a Rose

Yes, I'm a rose with many thorns
Although no heart will ever mourn
Even when pricked by careless tricks
For my love is gracious without scorn
My beauty possesses honor by itself

Essence is greater than carnal wealth
Sophistication never moves in stealth
Beauty of my soul the mystery untold
Precious flower of every man's desire
Beholds the wisdom of a King's attire

My thorns protect, come at your own risk
No matter how many times he's pricked
Comes back for more, I'm truly adored
Soft as velvet and devotion like a dove
A rose is bold & will always be loved

The Heart of a Rose

Love loss

He left me alone
yet sits beside me.
He hears my words
yet has not listened.
He lit my heart on fire
yet without any warmth.
My days are passing
yet time is standing still.
It feels like I am alone
yet he is never gone.
What possibly can I do?
This love isn't fulfilling
nor any longer true.

The Heart of a Rose

I gave you sunshine
You brought the rain
I gave you sweetness
You brought me pain
I gave you my heart
You tore it right apart
I gave you my time
You were out of line
I gave you goodbye
You told too many lies

Winds of Change

The Heart of a Rose

I know you love roses
but let me be your Sunflower.
I will show you what
sunflowers can do.

I will be your sunshine
because yellow is true.
I'll brighten your days and
love you in every way.

I'll make you forget that you
were bruised by a thorn.
Gentle and meek is
what you'll find in me.

Maybe a sunflower is the
love of your final destiny.

The Heart of a Rose

I chose you for me...

To be in love for eternity,
as my soul sings to be free.
Ecstasy became a reality,
and no longer just an unseen dream.

Loving you became hard,
I only wanted to be a salve for your scars.
To soothe you and make you forget,
that you were ever hurt.

I know true love is foreign,
and trust has been distant.
Pure love holds no burden,
and is never inconsistent.

If you let your guard down,
with confidence in me—
I promise to be your queen,
and shine brightly for all to see.

The Heart of a Rose

It never mattered to me that we
are cut from two different cloths.
I'm drawn to the heat of your
flame like a moth.

I see the depths of your
heart through your eyes.
Embracing the truth—
my feelings are not a lie.

I may not be your familiar type,
yet I'll be your comfort in the night.
Words can never express that I'm
the meaning of love in your life.

My passion for you is undying
and without measure.
You lower my inhibitions
with a kiss—it's my pleasure.

I'm in love with you

The Heart of a Rose

In silence
I heard your cry
and wiped your
tears with a prayer;
releasing the burden
of your weeping heart.
I am the glue for your
broken parts and the
love you'll embark.

The Heart of a Rose

Let's get naked...

Like the bare way
you came into the earth
Let me see your private parts
and what they're worth

Strip down to your insecurities
I want to know how big you are endowed
Does it measure the size of your heart?
I want to see the true colors of your art

Undress the depths of my mind
Show me, open up wide to the divine
Place your thoughts upon mine
Disrobe, so I can see you in our hardest times

The Heart of a Rose

Your touch is
the warmth that
soothes my soul.

Your kiss is
the desire of my heart.

Touching my mind
is where to start.

To attain the keys
to unlock the door
to a deeper part.

The Heart of a Rose

The Heart of a Rose

The love I have for you
is like no other.
It's pure, genuine, and
from the depths of my soul.
I know love has not been
your friend in the past.

Stay with me and I will show
you how it's meant to last.
I need you to trust me
with your heart to become
one and never part.
I'll keep your secrets and
turn back the clock.

Your slate is clean with
me and a fresh start.
I'm not the one who hurt
you or tarnished your worth.
I'm the one who loves you
and will witness your rebirth.

The Heart of a Rose

The Heart of a Rose

If I fail to see tomorrow,
I would kiss you more
today even if there was
some time to borrow.

I would hold you more
today even though the
time lines are narrow.

My heart will never
die or feel any sorrow.
Your love gives me
hope to see tomorrow.

The Heart of a Rose

The depths of the sea
You will find hidden in me
I'll show you fantasy and
Maybe even a wet dream
Let me take you for a swim
Surely your tide will rise...

The sky is near and blue
As the water engulfs you
Sun glistens on your skin
Feel the ocean from within
My love keeps you alive
Surely your tide will rise...

As the current is strong
Breathe deep all day long
Quench my desire of thirst
I'll be your last and the first
Baptise me with passion
Surely your tide will rise…

As the sun sets and dims
Your kiss will bring you in
I exhale love as we begin
Even if you can not swim
Please don't say goodbye
Surely your tide will rise...

Sounds of Poetry

The Heart of a Rose

Poetry is like…
Sipping on a glass of wine,
while relaxing in the midnight hour
after a long hot shower.
Taking you to a place inside of
your mind, maybe even another time.
To read it, is to embrace.
And to write it, is grace.
Nonetheless it takes you
into another place.

The Heart of a Rose

A Poet bleeds the ink from within
so let the words I write sink in.
If full of distortion you'll read a
portion of the madness inside.
If full of hurt you will see how
the ink bleeds deep into the dirt.
If full of compassion you'll read
words written in warmly fashion.

If full of turmoil the ink bleeds
how milk will quickly spoil.
If full of romance the words
sweetly make your heart dance.
If full of adventure the ink bleeds
pleasure with keen endeavors.
If versatile the words are written
interestingly worth your while.

A Poet bleeds from deep within
so let the words I write sink in.
If full of love the words will heal
and a message will be revealed.
If full strife the words are a fight;
nonsense is hard to understand.
Writing soothes the soul, so I'll
bleed purpose with pen in hand.

The Heart of a Rose

SHE

There's mystery in her eyes,
yet they do not lie.
Softly spoken are her words,
yet they pierce like a knife.
Her lips are dignified and
her tongue bears no strife.
She moves with charisma &
wears charm on her right arm.
She walks in integrity and
holds loyalty in her bosom.
She loves and seeks wisdom.
Her intellect intrigues
and moves like the wind—
Surely, she is a true friend.

Memories

As the rain dances
against the window pane—
I glare and begin to reminisce
of the times we spent laughing;
even the nights we went dancing.

You were my first love
and I never imagined there
would be one above.

Oh, but young ladies grow up
and things certainly do change.
Nonetheless I thought of you;
as the rain danced on the window pane.

The Heart of a Rose

If I was a painting...

I'd be a Picasso and possess
how the eyes see beauty.
I'd be the colors that soothes the soul.

I'd be the boldness that meets the canvas.
I'd be the richness of expression from
the start, to bring out the passion for art.

I'd be a masterpiece of exuberance
which makes the eyes dance merrily.
My colors would display hues of clarity.

I'd be my own exhibit on display for
all to see—red, blue, orange, and green.
If I was painting that's what I'd be.

A Picasso bold and strikingly.

The Heart of a Rose

Mosaic

If I was broken and chipped,
Would you still want me?
Would you still consider me
a valuable piece of art?
Would you still see me as
beautiful in all my many parts?
Could you pick up the pieces
without fear of being cut?
Could you place each piece intricately,
so I can become your mosaic masterpiece?
On display for the whole world to see...

The Heart of a Rose

The Heart of a Rose

I am in love with the
beautiful things in life.

A soft yellow flower
growing in the meadow.
The dewdrops on the
leaves of a sycamore tree.

The way the clouds
move beneath the stars
in the midnight hour.
A lily pad floating in
a nearby pond.

The sweet smell of
a honeysuckle vine
growing on a picket fence.
Yeah, I'm in love with the
beautiful things in life.

The Heart of a Rose

The Heart of a Rose

I saw a man while strolling in
the park yesterday, and he just
happened to look my way.
Little did I know by looking into
his eyes, that I would find what
I was longing for deep inside.

He was a charmer yet honest
with integrity very pristine.
He was authentic in every way,
unlike any man I'd ever seen.
Some say love at first sight
is merely just a fairytale dream.

Although on that day,
God's light had shined upon me
and I began to clearly see.
The perfect man that will give
his love through all eternity.

The Heart of a Rose

If dewdrops could speak what
exactly would they say to me?
Maybe they'd whisper a tale of
how the earth is void of unity.

Possibly tell me how the
forests are dying so rapidly.
Maybe even tell me the secret
plan for the earth's ecology.

Nonetheless if they could speak;
Maybe they would tell me of
God's love for our eternity.

Betrayal

I'll pick up my cross even
though it was never mine to bear.
The treachery of others have
left me broken and in despair.
Truth is bitter and tastes like fire;
to those who are habitual liars.
Kissing the lips of death;
Why do they put God to the test?
The time is soon to come
when my blood will be avenged
The heartbreaking part is...
My killers are my friends.

Melancholy

Daytime is searching through the
night as if it belongs to the dark.
Memories of the elusive things
are the destination mark.

Hoping to feel substance in
the air but it's not there.
As every second passes,
I realize the smell of despair.

Pressing through the dark,
may possibly be my destiny.
Will I walk this path for eternity?
Hope, please be my friend
and guide me to the end.

The Heart of a Rose

If kindness were a coveted commodity,
wouldn't the people want to buy it?
It seems like it's a character trait
unknown to the human race.

Long forgotten and its absence
has become a disgrace.
Brutal wounds of the neglected and
weeping sorrows of the desperate.

Beckoning the call of injustices and
relinquishing its place in the world.
Kindness, please come back to us
and grab a hold on love.

A Rose Scorned

The Heart of a Rose

Waiting for prince charming
to sweep me off my feet is
a fairytale I'll never meet.
A wish upon a darkened star;
is what love has shown me so far.
For every love I seemed to know...
He turned out to be a painful woe.

The Heart of a Rose

There's nowhere to hide when you're dying inside.
Emotions burning through my veins...
From the heartbreak that came, causing my deepest pain.
No signs of remorse or even the slightest care;
how he could bring me to such despair.
Nevertheless I feel free and my heart will heal.
He'll never truly understand the depths
of my love, or how I feel.
I believe in love and will never give up hope.
Someday I'll find the one who makes me
forget my heart ever broke.

The Heart of a Rose

My heart bleeds from the
silent stabs of neglect.
Like a rose left to wither and die;
cut off from being loved.
Petals fade and drop away—
hoping for nourishment or a brighter day.
To love me is to cherish and preserve.
Is it a rose that he deserves?
I am cut in all my beauty and splendor.
Yes, there are thorns but I'm still tender.

The Heart of a Rose

Poisoned with the strychnine of your ways
As they seep deep throughout my veins
Exactly how does this story begin?
With you being a selfish soul within
Let my side of the story be told...

Nights left alone and no one to care
While you were out running here and there
Why do I see neighbor women looking at me?
Because you sleep with them too secretly

Trust is gone and every promise broken
What use to be true is now long forgotten
Thought you would be my dream come true
Now I despair in this matrimonial nightmare

Deceitful Lover

Oh, what a tangled web he weaved,
when first he practiced to deceive—
as the lies spun so crafty to appease.
Binding his prey in a very subtle way.

Trapped in the delusion of his world,
is where he seems to entangle his girl.
Corners of his mind is where secrets lie.
Just a little bit longer to bide some time.

As the deceptions pile high to the sky.
Truth comes as light to expose his lies.
Oh, little skillful spider that you are—
My wisdom will burn your web from afar.

The Heart of a Rose

I'm drowning in disappointment
My love boat has been sunken
From the love I thought was true
My heart has been broken

He tested the waters and realized
They were much too deep
Didn't steer to give me hope
Not even an anchor to keep me

Couldn't tread and wouldn't swim
He just let the stormy water in
So we both drowned in the
disappointment from the waves

The Heart of a Rose

Wishing I could turn back
the hands of the clock.

To a time when our love was
perfect and without faults.

When you possessed the key
to the vault of my heart.

A perfect love gone wrong;
like a tune of a very sad song.

The love we shared, shattered
by your scandalous affair.

The Heart of a Rose

The Heart of a Rose

If yesterday was tomorrow...

I would have trusted you a little less
So that the next day I'd be blessed
Instead of wondering why the love
I shared with you was put to a test

Those things which I believe were true
Turned out to be the lies within you

Is there a man who walks in honesty?
Maybe hope is just a mere frivolity
Trusting you brings me to my knees
I pray to be healed wholeheartedly

The Heart of a Rose

And then she knew…
to lose him
would heal her pain
to let him go
would ease her mind

Moments in Love

The Heart of a Rose

I miss your touch
I miss your appeal
I miss the way you feel
I miss the time we had
I miss the enticing thrill

I need you immensely
I need you close to me
I need to kiss you merely
I need to hear your voice
I need to hold you dearly

love you

The Heart of a Rose

Maybe if we start over again
it would be different.
This time around you'll know
and understand the mistakes
before they happen.

Maybe you will know the wrongs
and remember what caused my pain.
Maybe you will clearly see
the love inside of me.

The beauty I bestow in warmth
and my gentleness will shine
like the noonday sun to you.
Maybe we can talk about the
things you kept hidden.

Spending more time together and
your love won't be fair-weathered.
Maybe we could restore what was lost.
If we start over again it would be different.

The Heart of a Rose

All I ever wanted is to love you,
to prove that integrity is true.
To make you feel warm at home,
even in the coldest of storms.
To give you the desires of your heart,
but trusting me is where you must start.
Your destiny is important to me
and I will help you to achieve.
Together is our power, love is our bond.
Every day we empower each other
and our newness stays strong.
My love isn't the one who broke you,
it's the one who has chosen you;
to be mine until the end of time.

The Heart of a Rose

You give me the reason to
trust being in love again.
You make me feel safe to
know you'll never leave.

Your touch is satisfying
and fulfills my needs.
Your love makes me weak
yet gives me strength.

You never leave me to
wonder or in suspense.
You give me the reason
to love without pretense.

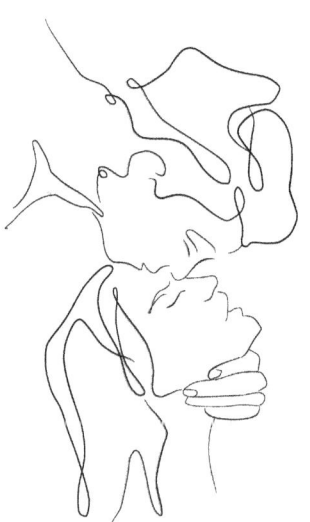

The Heart of a Rose

Your love for me
is like a honeycomb—
sweetness to my soul and
health to my bones.

With you I feel
comfort and the peace that
only one could dream of.
Many have come yet no
one can compare to you.
Every day our love
feels brand new.

You are the
morning sun and my
days will always be bright.
My lover, my friend, my
sanctuary at night.

Mr. Majestic

Lover of my soul and
the apple of my eye.
Intensity and warmth
as I lay in your arms.

Pulling me deeply in
with your subtle charm.
You are my safe place
to be without any harm.

Chocolate candy kisses
could never compete
with the sweetness that
you gently give to me.

You are my pleasure
which is mine to give.
Without your love is a
place I will never live.

The Heart of a Rose

The Heart of a Rose

I love you like bumble bees and trees
I'll give you honey but I'll never sting

You will always be the nectar I crave
I'll sprinkle pollen on you every day

I'll provide you with soothing shade
And the sun will never scorch

But just enough heat to light your torch
I'll be the dewdrops moistening your leaves

I'll be the wind that keeps the wood hard
The sap that oozes down your bark

Under the tree is my favorite spot
I'll rest my wings when the days are hot

The Heart of a Rose

The Heart of a Rose

The sweat of your brow
tells me you are pleased;
as I dance inside while
you move with ease.

Holding you closely is
the pinnacle of heights;
that we soar conveying
sounds of a tigers roar.

Every moment I kiss you
leaves me wanting more.
If passion was a place of
rest you could reside in
the depths of my breast.

Never will you know the
meaning of having less.
The love I give you will
keep you at your best.

The Heart of a Rose

Come my love,
Take me to the place we go.
Where no one knows.
Only you can bring me there.
I will meet you at the spot.
Wait for me if I get there too soon.
But I will never be too late.
Only you can bring me to the place.

Symphony of a Rose

The Heart of a Rose

Play music with your words
on my heart like a harp.
Slow dance me with the
rhythm of your thoughts.

Sway me by the melody
of your rhyme, I'm certain
I will have an exquisite time.

Romancing me with
your smooth baritone—
whisper to me all night long.

The Heart of a Rose

I'm going to dream about you tonight
And hope that you meet me there
Before closing my eyes I begin to drift...
And smell your scent in the atmosphere
Which causes me to fall fast asleep
Then my dream becomes my fantasy

Yet it's still a mystery
Because actually it's our reality
You showed me which way to go
To know pure ecstasy....
And together we will journey
Towards each other's destiny

Music plays like a soft symphony
Angels sing in perfect harmony
Doves dance in the sky flying high
As I look deep into your eyes...
The morning brings comfort to me
Knowing you are all I ever need

The Heart of a Rose

My heart skips a beat as I
come close to you.
Your lips are like the taste
of chocolate fondue.

Your eyes have the depths
of the Black sea.
When I look into them it's
tantalizing for me.

The tone of your voice
is music to my ears.
Romantic and like reading
a poem by Shakespeare.

My imagination runs wild
even when you smile.
Your kiss is the spark that
ignites my heart.

The Heart of a Rose

Where the wind blows, no one knows
but where my lover goes—I will follow.

The Heart of a Rose

I love him so much...
I could let him go and be free,
To fly away to his destiny.
To soar the sky and say goodbye.

I may even cry,
But in bondage I will never let him die.
Even if the storms come,
He'll remember me as his cover.

If he gets cold,
He'll remember that I am warmth;
If he gets hungry out on his own,
He'll remember I nourished him.

And if he encounters another,
He'll always remember I am his lover.
If he gets thirsty,
He'll taste the waters of the sea.

If it's salty and destiny is just a dream.
Flying wasn't what he expected it to be.
Maybe he will come back to me.
Knowing I loved him enough to be free!

The Heart of a Rose

The Heart of a Rose

Your pain is my pain
I feel the same
My love is your love
No one's above
I know your heart
From the start
Nothing can divide
Our love apart

The Heart of a Rose

A Purple Rose

Mysterious & unknown
Beauty of the royalties
No man has truly seen

A precious love pristine
Honor and grace within
Melodies of a symphony

Sweet music to his ears
A love bringing no tears
Warmth and gentleness

Comfort softly bestowed
Kisses of velvet pleasure
Patience without measure

Darkness is always calm
A purple rose in his arms

The Heart of a Rose

The Heart of a Rose

Listen to my heartbeat
What are the words it speaks?
It's your warm love that it seeks
Your touch makes me so weak
Soaring high in the midnight sky

For you, It's my prize…

Fantasies are bliss,
When I feel your kiss
Let's come together & escape
To where no one knows,
As we embrace the shining stars

The moon speaks our language
Your touch is my magic wand
No one else it's bestowed upon
Forever is a seven letter word
Majestically sweet and superb

The Heart of a Rose

If I was blind,
I would still see
you in my future.

If I was deaf,
I would surely hear
the melody of your love.

The Heart of a Rose

Special Thanks

To the love of my heart
who wrote this poem for me.

From one kiss on a rose
You are definitely the one I chose
Collecting your essence on that soulful glory
Spending time preparing for holy matrimony
Your fragrance lights up the room
As I become your shining groom
Fixing our hearts on that eternal seal
Flowing to the portrait of eternity's field
A duty that clings to the quality
Of honoring that newly journey
Of savoring that long lasting adventure
To measure the strength of each texture
Amazing growth from the seeds we throw
Tasting loads of deeds to sow
Never forsaking our roles as we need to show
True efforts of taking our leads for tomorrow
Laying my life to the protection
Of calling you wife in that direction
Of satisfying highs upon sections
Of soaring the skies with vivid renditions

The Heart of a Rose

Pleasant words are as a honeycomb,
sweet to the mind and healing to the body.

Proverbs 16:24

The Heart of a Rose

www.ingramcontent.com/pod-product-compliance
Lightning Source LLC
Chambersburg PA
CBHW042342300426
44109CB00048B/2695